C000264177

STEEL CITY

This first edition published in 2021 by Steel City Press,
9 Ravenscroft Close, Sheffield, S13 8PN.

Now I See
ISBN 978-1-913047-17-7

CONTENTS

Dedication

To my wife Hilary, with the most enormous thanks for putting up not just with me, but with the many stresses and strains caused by my loss of eyesight over many years.

Acknowledgements

I would like to take this opportunity to express my sincere thanks to my family, friends , colleagues, churches, the eye department at the Royal Hallamshire Hospital, and the S.R.S.B. for their support and inspiration at incredibly challenging times, You have helped to give me the strength to carry on.

Chapter 1 - Growing Pains

*"Well, I should not have thought it strange
That growing causes growing pains
'Cause the more we learn the more we know
We don't know anything"*

- Lyrics by Carolyn Arends

When I was a child, people would say that you could always tell someone from Scunthorpe: the faint smell of the steelworks seemed to linger wherever you went. In 1086, the town of Escumesthorpe was recorded in the Domesday Book: the town is coming up to its first millennium of known history. It probably dates from even further back than that - Roman burials and ruins are frequently discovered in the North Lincolnshire area.

The town has a rich but untapped history, a quaint mix of heavy industry and picturesque gardens, creating a unique sense of charm. I grew up on Highfield Avenue, a stone's throw away from the hospital and close walking distance to the Old Show Ground where Scunthorpe United used to play their home games.

I was born, as I would later learn, because my parents wanted a companion for my older sister Pauline - who has indeed been a lifelong friend. Many of my best childhood memories involve her, but if anything it's the little things which stick in the mind: my child-like delight that she allowed me to put the letters into the postbox when we went to mail out our Christmas cards, which for a young boy seemed like the most amazing thing in the world.

When I first started at the junior school, I didn't know where the toilets were. Being too embarrassed to ask, I would always make sure to wait until I got home. One day, the inevitable accident happened. I couldn't possibly admit to it.

For a 5-year-old, the only course of action was to brave it out, and try to cover it up. Unfortunately, the teacher - who rather resembled Margot in the Good Life, all prim and proper - immediately noticed upon entering the room. "Oh, what an awful smell!", she pronounced, and lined us all up in order to determine the culprit.

When she came to me, she immediately exclaimed *"Oh! Oh! Oh!"*

Telling me how disgusting I was, and instructing me to "Get Out", she pushed me to the front door. I remember standing outside the classroom looking lost in the corridor until someone found me, cleaned me up, put me some clean clothes on and sent me home early. I remember being absolutely mortified - and making sure that I found out where the toilets were, so I never had the same problem again.

One day, our class was tasked with making a paper aeroplane and decorating it with crayons. In those days, the distinctive bullseye-style concentric circular patterns which you'd see on an old-fashioned Spitfire were the order of the day. I spent an hour or so decorating it, before we were told that we could go and play with them outside. I was delighted that it actually flew, until a gust of wind took it and it went into the big boys' playground. One large boy asked "Is this your aeroplane?". When I said that it was, he stomped on it, twisting his foot on it and destroying it mindlessly. I was so upset: not just at losing my newly-prized possession, but by my realisation of just how nasty children could be to others.

School wasn't always quite so negative. As was always the case at every primary school in the 1960s, we would be expected to draw plenty of pictures. I was still 5 years old, but now in the next class. I recognised that other children would simply put a strip of blue and draw a sun. That would be the sky. But I looked out of the window, and seeing the scene outside I chose instead to draw a picture of clouds against the blue sky as background.

I wrote "This is the sky, and the clouds are drifting across the sky". The teacher was so happy, encouraging me and saying just how descriptive I was. Perhaps, even then, I was imagining that I would love to be an author one day.

My grandfather died when I was around six or seven years old, and my grandmother insisted that we all went to live with her - which was a great bonus for the family finances! She had an obsession with pianos, having a huge concert grand piano and an upright piano in her small semi-detached house.

I remember walking into the room, and my grandmother pointed a finger at me before declaring "He's going to learn to play the piano". I had no choice in the matter, and neither did my parents. I was sent forthwith to the local piano teacher, with no possible argument being brooked. She even bought me a brand-new piano of my own. I eventually got a Grade 8 in piano, doing well in competitions. It turned out to be a real blessing later in life, because even when I lost my sight I was still able to continue to play.

The first time I had any clue that there might be something amiss with my eyesight was at the age of six. I recall queuing up with my classmates to get our eyes tested. The nurse handed me pieces of cardboard. As she held up each shape, the task was simple enough - I merely had to hold up the corresponding shape. As I failed to complete this task, she started to become more and more angry. Thinking back now, I suspect it wasn't real anger but just her way of determining which child actually had a sight problem - and which child simply wasn't paying attention.

One way or the other, I'd failed the school eye test and a letter was despatched to my parents with haste. They were told that I needed to visit an optician. Unsurprisingly, the optician diagnosed short-sightedness in both eyes and recommended that I should wear glasses permanently.

At around the same age, I developed nephritis in my kidneys - which kept me off school for about six months. To my shock, when I went back to school I was put in a higher class. My birthday was on August 30th, right on the cusp between two year groups. Until this point they had made a mistake, putting me in the lower year group as though my birthday had been in September. But when I went back to school they corrected their mistake, moving me into the next year group up. I started to believe that I was stupid because I was unable to catch up with the year above having also lost an additional six months of my education through illness. It was another seven years before I finally realised exactly what had happened.

I was now seven years old, and had lost a massive amount of weight because of the nephritis. I had my new specs on, and all the boys were playing a newly-invented game called 'football' which I hadn't a clue about. On top of this, I wasn't allowed to participate in games or physical education classes as I was considered too thin and fragile. Under the circumstances, looking back today it is hardly surprising that I often found myself rejected by the other boys in the class who didn't like the look of me, and when I asked if I could play with them they always said "No".

The only children who would play with me were the girls. It didn't take me very long to learn the practical lesson that boys hit you and weren't very nice, but girls were much more accommodating. They would even share their sweets with me and allow me to join in their games or marbles. I found myself having to play in the girls' playground. My dad's attempts to toughen me up, by buying me a pair of boxing gloves and a punchbag, ended in me throwing the gloves down onto the floor and storming up to my room. That just wasn't me.

My later childhood was often rough and ready, as would be expected of those who attended Scunthorpe's Secondary Modern school. My dad was a steel worker, the archetypal rough ex-army hands-on type but with a fierce intellect behind it. He was the ultimate macho man, but thanks to my illness I was a very delicate child. It was certainly an unusual mix in our family background.

When I went to Scunthorpe Secondary Modern, swear words were the order of the day but I never really wanted to take part in that kind of thing. "Why", the other children would ask me, "don't you swear like everyone else?" Those who were different would always be likely targets for bullies - and I had a terrible bully when I first started at the school.

When I complained to my dad, the advice I received was unsurprising and uncompromising: "Hang the b***** on. You don't let them touch you, you smash his face in". This advice wasn't really within my comfort zone, but eventually the provocation was just too much.

I snapped, punched him full in the face just as my dad had suggested, and he fell over backwards in front of all the rest of my class. "Skippy's thumped Hug Hess" (his name was Hughes), was the cry which rang around the school. Hug Hess was an absolutely classic bully, made in the stereotypical mould. He was very large and hairy, but it transpired that he didn't much like actually being punched himself. He continued to bully everyone else but he never touched me ever again.

Even now, so many years later, I can still remember that punch. I had no skill in fighting - but I just did it. Whenever I hear the story of David and Goliath, I always secretly chuckle to myself.

The education was fairly brutal. One of the teachers would line us all up, lifting our aprons, and whack us with the steel ruler with (or sometimes without) the slightest justification. Although it was horrendous, in a way it actually strengthened me.

Misery can often do that: it gives you the Scunthorpe steel you need to be able to cope with whatever life throws at you - and life has certainly thrown a lot at me.

Chapter 2 - Like riding a bike

*"Ride, baby, ride
Lessons in life are going to show you in time
Soon enough you're gonna know why
It's gonna hurt every now and then
If you fall get back on again"*
Lyrics by Ronnie Dunn and Terry McBride

It was 1957 and the family had gone on holiday to a caravan site in Mablethorpe. The first day, I held my dad's hand and we walked around the caravan park. We came to a bike hire shop full of every kind of bicycle possible, and it was full of excited children hiring the bikes and riding them - and obviously having great fun.

Then I said "Dad, can I have one? I want to ride a bike."

He replied "No, you're not big enough". I insisted - and, unusually for my dad, he gave in and hired a small bike that was just my size.

I was four years old at the time. We went on to a grassy field next to the shop, he lifted me on to the bike and told me to put my feet on the pedals. I pedalled furiously, determined to ride my bike like the big boys and girls. Dad was running alongside me and holding me. Then he let go of me, and I was riding a bike on my own! It was so exciting, but I realised I didn't know how to get back off it again. The only way was to stop pedalling and then I would fall off onto the grass. I got up and said "Again!".

Falling off was all part of the fun. That afternoon, dad spent the whole time putting me on the bike, running with me, and then letting me go. Then when I wanted to, I would stop pedalling and would fall off.

Afterwards, we went into a 1950s-style milk bar. It was full of brightly-coloured metal chairs around tables, with a juke box playing records in the corner. The waiters were frying onions and sausages, making hot dogs. There were bottles of different kinds of milkshake syrups, hanging upside down around the bar. The combination of the hot dog smell and colourful milkshake syrups was an intoxicating sensory overload to a young child, etching the moment indelibly into my memory.

Dad bought me a hot dog, and asked what flavour milkshake I would like. I said strawberry, and we both sat there eating and drinking: for that one moment, I thought I had the best dad in the world. He was obviously proud of me, that I could now ride a bike.

As I grew up, for various reasons our relationship began to sour. Although I did well at school, nothing I did ever seemed to quite be good enough for him. It seemed as though he felt that giving praise was unhelpful: if I finished second in the class, he would wonder why I wasn't first. I felt that I could never please him - no matter what I did, the bar was always raised even higher.

As a young man, once I'd left home the relationship had deteriorated. My mother had died a few years before, and I recall phoning him and getting no response. I spoke with my sister, who assumed that my dad had just gone away somewhere with his new girlfriend. I didn't rush over there, in case it would cause him any embarrassment.

Then the phone rang. It was the hospital; my dad had been rushed in after suffering a stroke. I headed straight over there, and I could immediately see just how ill he was. The nurse gave me a feeder cup with some tea in it to give him. I put my arm around him and lifted the cup to his mouth so that he could drink. At that moment, all the stupid misunderstandings between us were gone. A week or so later, he sadly passed away.

I'll forever choose to remember him, frozen in time, in that field in Mablethorpe. For one day, in 1957, he was the perfect father. Today, I hope, I would be his perfect son.

Chapter 3 - Coincidences?

"When I pray, coincidences happen, and when I don't, they don't" - William Temple, Archbishop of Canterbury (1942-1944)

At the age of 20, I went to university in Reading. In the first year I studied physiology and biochemistry, then microbiology and chemistry. After the first three terms, I'd choose which of them to pursue at degree level. From the first day, I realised that I'd made a terrible mistake. I loathed everything about it, but in those days I felt rather stuck in it: not many people from my Secondary Modern background would have such an opportunity to succeed academically.

I was completely out of my comfort zone, down South with a Scunthorpe accent which people could barely understand. They seemed to think that I lived in a little terraced house in a backstreet somewhere with whippets in the back garden and pigeons in the loft.

I recall at one university meal, seeing the North-South divide placed into particularly stark context. There was some sort of paste on the table, which didn't look particulatly appetising. "What's that?", I asked - only to receive the slightly bemused response "pate, I think". Southerners might well have pate; us Northerners required no pretensions beyond mere potted meat!

Deep down inside, I knew that I was in the wrong place. I was with the wrong people, studying the wrong course at the wrong university. There are moments in life when you just know that something really needs to change - and this was one of them. It still wasn't quite clear, though, what else I could do.   If there was one thing I sorely needed, it was some clarity in my life.

My life changed, surprisingly, with a knock on the door. Would I like, asked the person at the other side, to take a look at the Bible? At a time when I was desperately searching for answers, the answer was delivered straight to my door. He signposted me to the Gospel of St. John - and in particular the phrase where Jesus describes himself: "I am the Way, the Truth and the Life". Matthew, Mark and Luke - the so-called 'synoptic' gospels - approach Jesus' life in a same way. John is different: it contains many of the same stories, but instead of focusing on *what* Jesus did, it focused on *who* He is.

From that day, something changed in my life. I couldn't put my finger on it at the time, but with God at the centre my life now had a clear purpose. There were twelve of us who were believers at around this time - ironic, we thought, given the importance of the number twelve in the Bible (think of the twelve disciples for example). At that time, university halls of residence didn't have the kind of support available which they do now. Many of us were feeling quite lonely, or even a little lost, so we were surprised when we invited people to meetings that they actually turned up!

Over my time in Reading I became involved with church, developing Christian friends, and met a lovely young man from the Seychelles who lived opposite and just happened to be doing the same course as me. He was so enthusiastic about his chosen career - dentistry - that I started to give it serious consideration. It's strange how, from such chance meetings, our lives can take such a dramatically different turn. The more I thought about it, the more I was drawn to dentistry.

Because of my grades being so good, I was able to get into dental school for the following year without even so much as an interview. It was off to Liverpool for a fresh start, and a career in dentistry.

Before heading back up North, I spoke to my mother, who was still alive at the time. She said "You need to come back home and get some money before going to dental school".

My mother had a friend who worked at the Nypro chemical plant in Flixborough, and she offered to arrange me a job in order to help me save money to pay my way through university.

Over the next few days, I gave the matter serious consideration - but the more I thought about it, and especially when I started to pray about it, the more uneasy I became. I knew for sure that I wasn't supposed to go to Flixborough, though for the life of me I couldn't possibly have explained why.

When I told my mum that I wouldn't be coming back for a summer job, she slammed the phone down on me: she couldn't understand why I'd turn down the chance to earn some money and enjoy some family time back home with her. I wasn't fully sure that I understood either.

June 1ˢᵗ, 1974.

The leaking no.5 reactor at the Nypro chemical plant was bypassed two months ago after a 6-foot crack was found in the reactor's steel shell. Other leaks having been dealt with, the plant was brought back up to usual temperature and pressure. A massive release of flammable cyclohexane vapour in the vicinity of reactor no.5 lead to a massive explosion at the plant. 2,000 nearby homes are damaged.

Of the 72 people on site that day, 28 were killed and a further 36 seriously injured. It was the largest ever peacetime explosion in the United Kingdom. It made my mother think, to the extent that she later told me "I believe in Jesus" because of what had happened.

I don't know how to process all of the emotions that come from an incident like that: knowing that I could have so easily been there, had I made a different decision. The explosion shook the country, but especially the community of Scunthorpe. It's a tragedy which is still felt deeply in the local area to this day, over 45 years later. It was a senseless accident, a tragedy which is so difficult to understand - let alone explain. We live in an imperfect world, a world in which such horrific things can happen.

From my first day in Liverpool, I felt much more positive: I knew I was in the right place, training for my chosen career. I met other believers at the Freshers Fair, who were so warm and welcoming that I immediately felt at home and settled in without hesitation - in sharp contrast to my time in Reading. The Gospel was spreading like wildfire on campus: people might have come originally for want of anything better to do, but they were basically listening to the good news of Jesus Christ. By the end of the year, there were 45 of us. It seemed that every week, someone would be telling us about a new person who had become a Christian. In fact,it all became something of a culture shock to me when I went back into a 'normal' church: I wasn't seeing people getting saved on a daily or weekly basis in quite the same way. There are, I'm sure, some lessons to be learned in that!

I recall one girl, who was slightly outside of my normal sphere of friends: a casual acquiantance, no more than a friend of a friend of a friend! She decided to get baptised, going along to a local church which had a baptismal tank. All of her student friends - a mixture of believers and non-believers - came. The believers were there to support her, and the non-believers turned up partly for the same reason - but also because they wanted to understand what was going on and why. The minister was shocked as over fifty new people turned up for the baptism, remarking that he "couldn't believe how many people had come to see you baptised".

On one occasion I just wanted the floor to swallow me up. I was chatting to another student who was worrying about his course: reading this, reading that, and wanting to make sure that everything was completed on time.Someone shouted across from the next table: "Reading? Well how about having your name *written* in the Lamb's book of life?"

A discussion of the finer points of Christianity followed. I apologised profusely to my friend afterwards: "Sorry about David!". "Actually, I thought it was fantastic", he responded - which took me aback. Clearly it was all part of a plan.

One thing is particularly close to my heart though. Christianity isn't just about what we believe about Jesus, it's also about our relationships with other people. Every night we would have a time where we'd meet in each other's rooms, talking about anything and everything - but also praying, praising and worshipping God on guitars, singing, and with whatever other instruments we might have to hand.

People realised that something extraordinary was happening, but in fact it was just normal. That's what Christianity should be like all the time. John 13:35 tells us that people should be able to tell that we're followers of Jesus by our love for one another: what a standard for us to live up to! I'm not going to quote the Bible very much in this book, but there is one passage which I just have to share because it sums up the whole situation:

"All the believers were together and had everything in common. They sold property and possessions to give to anyone who had need. Every day they continued to meet together in the temple courts. They broke bread in their homes and ate together with glad and sincere hearts, praising God and enjoying the favor of all the people. And the Lord added to their number daily those who were being saved." - Acts 2:44 - 47

That's what we're supposed to be. It was a genuine, bona-fide Christian revival - and we were grateful for the supportin prayer that was coming from all around the country.

One evening, I was at a party for students at university on New Year's Eve, 1979. I was chatting to a girl there who I'd known for a while, with no real expectation of anything romantic developing. The clock chimed midnight, and she turned to me with the words:

"Happy new decade!"

We looked at each other, and in that moment something clicked. That girl, Hilary, would later become my wife. As I'm writing this in 2020, fully forty years later, I remember asking her to say the same thing again as the new decade rolled round again - and it meant the world to me, reminding me of that day, when she said "Happy New Decade" to me once again.

The world moved on quickly: we got married, I found myself taking on a 'house' job at a hospital in Liverpool. It was the lowest rung on the ladder: crystal-clear to me that I was there to learn as I was taking out teeth whenever I wasn't acting as assistant for more complex dental surgery. After a couple of other jobs, I had the opportunity to move to Sheffield to take on a much more decent job.

It was a real step up, and a challenge which I was really looking forward to. For Hilary, it was a bit more challenging - she came across with me to a new city, not knowing anyone and not yet having found employment. I appreciated having her by my side as we embarked on our new journey together.

I was now a dentist working at a practice in the usual way - the kind of thing the average member of the public would have in their mind's eye when thinking about dentists.

Life, finally, was going well. Things were looking up and I had the metaphorical spring in my step when, in 1988, my first son was born.

I was married to a wonderful lady, had a great job, and now was father to a most beautiful baby boy, just a few months old. We were finally feeling much more settled in Sheffield. Aside from the ongoing short-sightedness in my left eye, corrected by my glasses, at 36 I was as fit as a fiddle. I could run the half-marathon in 1 hour 44 minutes.

Finally, I could relax! For the first time in my life, I could honestly say that I was truly happy.

Chapter 4 - Like pulling teeth

"My dentist told me I need a crown. I agree."

Whenever someone says that something is 'like pulling teeth', I have to smile: that was my job - in some ways, I did actually like pulling teeth and helping people to feel better. One of the great satisfactions in dentistry is when someone comes in, in absolute agony, and then leaves feeling much better. I recall one woman who had been months in pain from a severe toothache, being kept up all night regularly.

Her husband came up to me, got down on his knees and hugged me. "Thank God, thank God, you've done it!" - he was so pleased and so relieved that his ordeal was finally over. She followed me through into the waiting room, smiling, and everything was fine again.

There were some real characters in dentistry, starting right from the beginning at dental school. The first was a fantastic example of nominative determinism, a lecturer known as Emma Rotter - who was an expert at extracting rotten teeth. She was stunningly beautiful, a real Audrey Hepburn type with a wonderful Scandinavian accent.

Every time we had a problem extracting someone's tooth, the whisper would go around "Get Emma! Get Emma!" The scenes were often quite comical - a heavy docker-type, who'd seen three young and fit dental students unable to extract his tooth, would take one look at Emma as she came across, and would never believe that she could possibly do what they had all failed to. But she had mastered the technique - and with a swift flick of a wrist on the forceps, out would come the tooth. There's a real technique for taking teeth out, which really does develop over the course of a dental career. Emma was a fantastic example of just how easily appearances can be deceptive.

Part of the course was anatomy, and it involved cutting up dead bodies. I'm sure that to an outsider it would seem particularly revolting, but to us it was just normal, an expected part of the course. It was almost like cutting up a jelly baby: it was so pickled that it wasn't like a body at all. The medical students would do the torso; dental students would cut up the face. It taught us everything we needed to know, in the days before computerised models and simulations, about the muscles in the jaw and dental anatomy.

One of our lecturers, in periodontology, was a typical Yorkshireman. We had to learn all about gum disease, but he summed the whole thing up in one sentence: "scraping the crap off people's teeth". Despite endless tomes on the subject, everything could be explained so succinctly in just a few words. I can imagine, though, that using such a simple 'nutshell' explanation in a university examination wouldn't have gone down so well!

There was one moment when psychologically, things really changed for me. A bit like the green jacket in golf (U.S. Open) or the yellow jersey in the Tour de France, the first day that we went into the dental hospital wearing the white coat was a moment of real pride. To anyone outside looking in, it would have appeared for all the world like I was already a real dentist. After years of obtaining paper qualifications: O Levels, A Levels and so on, this was the moment when it finally felt tangible: I was actually going to qualify. "I'm a dentist now", I thought. Of course, it would be another four years before I *actually* qualified - but that first step was a real shot in the arm.

Tooth-coloured fillings. You'd drill a hole in the side of a tooth and fill it with tooth-coloured material. I showed my work to the lecturer, who criticised it as being too bulbous and the colour not being quite right. Unbeknownst to her, she was looking at the unfilled side of the tooth. She was criticising the normal tooth structure!

When I was newly-qualified, a man came in wanting some new teeth. We made them for him, but it left his teeth sticking out like Plug in the old children's comic *The Beano*. He was especially polite, asking "Don't you think they're sticking out a bit?" I responded by saying that he should give it a little time to "bed in", but it was an awful transformation. We had to redo the work a couple of weeks later. Thankfully dentistry (and my own skill) have progressed a long way since then.

As part of the process for putting in false teeth, there's a stage known as a 'try-in': the false teeth are there, but set in pink wax rather than plastic so that any needed adjustments can be made. One day, someone came in for what she thought was her new false teeth. Her somewhat overworked and rather tired dentist (a colleague, who I won't name to spare any blushes) got confused: the wax and the plastic look very similar. He thought that he was putting the final teeth in, but in fact he was doing the try-in. He sent her away.

It wasn't too long before the phone rang. His rather concerned patient told our practice that "I've just had a cup of tea, and all the false teeth have dropped off. What's wrong with my false teeth?"

It was the dentist's mistake, of course. The wax had melted, leaving her teeth to fall out. Thankfully, though, such comedic incidents were rare.

When I moved into the practice in Sheffield, a woman came in with gum disease. One of the features of gum disease is that it tends to cause teeth to stick out forwards because the bone is very weak. I told her that she needed to have her front teeth out, and that a denture would be needed. When you take the teeth out and make the denture, then - theoretically at least - they should automatically go back to the correct position as they 'bed in' over a period of time. In this case, they didn't. The plate was uncomfortable and didn't fit very well. She came back in a few weeks later, having eaten very little in the meantime. I was able to fix the problem.

In just a few weeks, her appearance had completely changed: she'd lost a lot of weight, and her teeth went from sticking out horribly to beautifully-aligned dentures. I could barely believe that it was the same person standing in front of me. She said "My life has been transformed by your skill" - praise which I appreciated very much, especially as it hadn't quite worked the first time.

There were many other comedic moments. When a patient is used to having a lot of tartar around their teeth, holes can appear between them when the tartar is scraped away. One of my colleagues had a patient who complained that "Seeds get stuck between my teeth now that the tartar has been removed".

Quick as a flash, the dentist replied "Now you know what birds feel like, Mrs. Smith!"

It reminded me of the old story of a lady who'd been to a Welsh chapel and heard a traditional hell-fire and brimstone type sermon referring to the wailing and gnashing of teeth in hell.

A member of the congregation approached the vicar, saying "I know you said in hell there'll be wailing and gnashing of teeth, but I've got false teeth".

The vicar wasn't going to let her off so easily, replying "They'll provide dentures."

Chapter 5 - Sight Loss

"Truth is, I CAN still laugh, smile, listen, talk, teach, dance, hug, love, and live happily. Vision loss can hold you down, but the truth will set you free."
– Maria Johnson, Girl Gone Blind

In the summer of 1989, I caught a dose of the flu. Like it had done several times before, it made me feel very ill. I took a couple of weeks off work, but by the end of the second week I felt fully recovered. I shrugged it off, returning to work at the start of the following week.

Something felt different though: whilst I was at work, I noticed that my good right eye seemed to be clouding over. It felt a little like when your glasses steam up, and needed to be cleaned. It happened mostly when I had my head over the patient, but only in the one eye.

I remarked to the dental nurse that it seemed strange, and as each day went by it seemed to mist up more and more. Then I noticed when driving at night little halos would appear around the street and car lights, which again I thought a little odd.

I asked a friend of mine, Gill, who was an optician to have a look at my right eye. She took one look at it, and immediately advised me that I should go to the eye department at the Hallamshire hospital. She was absolutely adamant and insisted that I could not brush it off, so I headed down there.

The diagnosis was inflammation in both eyes, but particularly in the right eye. It was ironic that of the two eyes, my right eye had always been the better one - yet it was the right eye which was much more affected by this. The diagnosis was uveitis. It causes inflammation, and the inflamed cells fill the eye from the inside. I was given steroid drops to be put in every two hours.

I'm no expert on the eye, so they explained it to me a little like one of those wonderful snow globes which you get at around Christmas time. When you shake the globe, the snow goes everywhere. Uveitis basically does the same thing within the eye. On its own, uveitis doesn't seem to be particularly bad - but the problem is that it caused other things to go wrong.

From my understanding, the eye has little drainage channels which drain the fluid from your eyeball. The cells blocked those drainage channels. It happened in both eyes, but was especially so in the right eye. The consequence was a build-up of pressure in my eyes, triggering glaucoma in both eyes - but especially so in my right eye. I was prescribed Timoptol drops for the glaucoma.

I also have allergic asthma. The Timoptol drops triggered an allergic reaction and severe asthma attacks. On one day, I went in gasping for breath - and the doctors recognised the issue, changing it to a different medication. Immediately, the asthma attacks stopped.

This became an ongoing battle for me because the glaucoma didn't clear up straight away, and everything gradually continued to deteriorate over the following years.

I started to disassociate myself from the symptoms. In the early stages, I simply thought that it was nothing to worry about and that it would all be fine in the end. I was very much enjoying life, so I considered this to be a temporary blip: a hump in the road which I needed to get over.

There was no particular pain or discomfort, just a nagging feeling that the sight in my right eye was fading across the whole visual field. This was slighty mistifying to the doctors, because glaucoma tends to take sight away from around the edge of the visual field and only taking the central vision after years of high pressure.

The lack of pain at that time (though believe me, it got worse later!) probably helped to lull me into a false sense of security: pain is the body's natural way of telling you that there is something seriously wrong. In the absence of any real discomfort, I was wrongly convinced that everything was going to be absolutely fine.

Still, the drops were not keeping the pressure down so the doctors decided to operate on both eyes in order to form an artificial drainage channel.

Whilst awaiting the operation, we went to Blackpool for a weekend - taking our baby son Daniel with us. In the early stages, my eye would cloud over temporarily but it would clear quickly. I was enjoying the break, and Daniel was lying in his cot in the hotel room.

Everything changed in an instant when I reached over to pick him up, and was suddenly devastated when I closed my left eye for a second and couldn't see him at all out of my right eye. In the early stages, the problem would clear up on its own. By this time it wouldn't clear at all.

The seriousness of the situation hit me like a lightning bolt.I was going blind. My hopes were now pinned on the operation.

A few weeks later, I went in for my first eye operation. The pressure in my eye dropped, and it became much more comfortable when I blinked. I felt positive about the outcome, but after a while the pressure gradually started to increase again. After a second operation, there was another temporary improvement - but before too long, I was back in the same place again.

They now offered me a laser treatment, which was designed to vapourise the ciliary body. They numbed the eye, and I could just hear a few clicks whilst they were performing the operation. They offered me a cup of tea and some toast; there was no pain whatsoever - until the point at which the anaesthetic started to wear off.

Suddenly, it felt like someone had put a red-hot poker into my eyeball. I can't even begin to explain just how bad it was. My entire body started to shake and tremble from the pain and I felt like I was going to vomit. As a dentist I'd never fully understood the debilitating nature of pain until this point: I'd seen patients come in, who were being destroyed by the pain of toothache. I suppose it was an example of the aphorism "if it hurts, it works".

The nurse said to me "I think you're getting yourself into a bit of a state". I certainly was, and I'd spotted a piano at the other side of the room. When I play the piano, it short-circuits the pain in a strange kind of a way. There was a piano in the room, and I asked to be allowed to play it. I started to play the piano in the waiting room, and it helped me to focus on something other than the pain. They gave me some painkillers, which eased it slightly, and I was able to go home.

It was quite a new procedure at the time. I think they now handle patients' pain much better, because it's much better understood now, but at the time it was brutal. But the pressure was still sky-high. The doctor said that they'd do yet another procedure, but I said no: after two trabeculectomies and one laser treatment, I didn't want yet another operation. At that point in time, there was no other treatment available for glaucoma - so it would have just been trying the same kind of thing again.

They wrote in my medical notes that "Mr. Skipworth has refused further treatment", and told me that I would likely go completely blind in that eye, but I thought that being pain-free was more important. I made an informed decision to have nothing further done to that eye.

In my now-sighted left eye, the pressure was going up as well: I had to have a trabeculectomy on that eye. The doctor was an Irishman, whose physical appearance didn't particularly inspire confidence in me - but the quality of his workmanship certainly did!

Every time I closed my eye, it felt as though there was irritation in it. It's that permanent sense of irritation which shows that the operation has worked: it's a surgical opening in the eyeball, known as a 'bleb', which allows the pressure to be relieved. The 'holy grail' of a trabeculectomy is to produce a good bleb.

If you've ever had something stuck in your eye, you'll have at least some idea of what it feels like. It worked well, but it affected everything - especially my sleep patterns: the only way I could go to sleep was to press my fingers firmly on the side of my head That way, I could trick my body into feeling that it knows the cause of the irritation - that my fingers were pressing there. Finally, I would be able to drop off to sleep.

At around this time, we were blessed with a second son, Joshua. People used to say that he was so much like my father: he looked just like him, and even had my dad's interest in more physical activities. I'm sure that my dad would have got on like a house on fire with Joshua. I think back to my dad's failed attempts to teach me to box: I just know that Joshua would have loved to learn!

I remember passing on my dad's advice about bullies to him - and Joshua was able to look after himself far better than I ever did. "That's one of the best bits of advice you ever gave me", he once told me, and I told him how the advice had filtered down from generation to generation.

Chapter 6 - None so blind

"None so deaf as those that will not hear. None so blind as those that will not see." - Matthew Henry

Years later, dental colleagues would remark how they could tell my dentistry as it was of a higher standard than normal NHS dentistry.

Private dentists would always wear loupes, which acted as a bit of a magnifying glass. Just like a good surgeon needs to see the operation they're carrying out in great detail, so too a dentist needs to see. If you ever need good dental surgery doing, then you should always go to a dentist who wears loupes.

I discovered this by accident: as my eyesight was failing, I had no choice but to start wearing loupes when I was unable to see well enough to do the job without them. By happy coincidence, the quality of the 'end product' of my dentistry improved.

With the risk of cross-infection, all dentists now wear gloves. This was never the case when I was first training, but it was brought in by the dental profession much later. We'd think nothing of it, washing our hands and any spots of blood away after the session. Thinking back today, I'm appalled that we did that - but it was just the way that things were done at the time. As our understanding of medicine improves, dentistry also develops. I often think that the dental profession should insist upon dentists wearing loupes, in much the same way that they now insist upon them wearing gloves.

When I first started dentistry, it was common to use gas for general anaesthetics on children - but after a number of issues, dentistry recognised that a local anaesthetic would be far better. At first, like many of my colleagues, I struggled to believe that young children would cope with local anaesthesia - but a lot of them were actually surprisingly good at dealing with it. I remember one little girl coming in, saying "I've got toothache". I asked her "Shall we take it out then?" and she immediately accepted it. I'd use words like "put the tooth to sleep". She went along with everything without a murmur and then asked me "Can I have a sticker now?". It was always best when the parents wouldn't make much of it, and as long as they stayed calm their children would also.

I felt that I was making the necessary adjustments to be able to work competently despite the loss of eyesight to that time. However, I was hit by another thunderbolt: overnight I was removed from the clinic I had worked at for the last twenty years. I was informed by management that I was changing clinics and going to a different one. There was obviously no choice in the matter, and I was given very little explanation by management. With hindsight, it all makes a little more sense: I couldn't drive any more because the DVLA were aware of the problem with my eyesight, so management were doubtless concerned that I would make a mistake and cause them a serious legal issue. It's understandable that they would have a fear about such things, though the standard of my work always spoke for itself!

The move to the new clinic was something of a concern to me, being whisked out of one environment to another. The new clinic had a bleak, austere feel to it. My line manager was changed, and I was forced to go through a period of months in which three dentists were observing every aspect of my clinical practice.

I was shocked by how poor the dental observers were. One of them was surprised I used dental X-ray positioners. Those positioners ensured that the X-ray was absolutely spot on, and essential at the time to practice good dentistry. I remember feeling quite concerned that someone who was there, sitting in judgment over me, wasn't using the best practice themself in their own dentistry.

The process continued for a good few months, but eventually I was given a clean bill of health and they were convinced that I was, in fact, giving a good standard of dental care to my patients.

I was hopeful that I could breathe a sigh of relief: there could no longer be any doubt about the quality of my work. However, despite their positive recommendation, my problems were only just beginning. Instead of having just one dental nurse working with me at the new clinic, I was working with a whole gang of dental nurses. Unbeknownst to me, they were all watching me - like a hawk.

I'd spent twenty years working in a positive environment, where colleagues trusted one another and worked together as a team. The atmosphere in this situation was completely different, with a constant sense of being watched. I was struggling to sleep, finding it difficult to eat properly, and lost a lot of weight over a number of months.

To me it seemed that many were keen to please the service and enhance their careers. What this group of nurses said about me nearly totally destroyed me as a human being, and if it hadn't been for my Christian faith I don't think

I would have been able to get through this time. In the middle of everything, there was one night when I couldn't find my pyjamas. It was looking like I was going to lose my job, get no money, and the sight in my good eye was going.

I turned to my Bible for inspiration, and immediately chanced upon Revelation 3:17-18:

"You say, 'I am rich; I have acquired wealth and do not need a thing.' But you do not realize that you are wretched, pitiful, poor, blind and naked. I counsel you to buy from me gold refined in the fire, so you can become rich; and white clothes to wear, so you can cover your shameful nakedness; and salve to put on your eyes, so you can see."

At the time I read those words I thought I was going to be poor. I was going blind, and - thanks to being unable to find my pyjamas - was naked as well. I certainly felt wretched and pitiful as well. Sometimes when you read the Bible, you find that the words just penetrate deep into your heart: at this point, I had that strong sense. Whilst my physical situation might have been particularly bad at the time, I knew that God had a plan. I found my pyjamas, so the nakedness went - but it was a few years after that before everything else was sorted. Now, though, I felt that something had changed: He had His hand on my life.

I had been summoned, completely out of the blue, to a meeting with the Manager, and my line manager. They handed me a document of complaints from the dental nurses with regards to my clinical practices.

I was shocked to the core by what these people had said. The spirit drained out of me and I slumped forward. My manager told me that I was suspended from work until further notice. My mouth went dry. I clutched the document I had been given which contained fifty complaints about my Clinical Practices. I saw a smile of satisfaction on my manager's face. You could fight two or three complaints, but fifty was a no-no. He was sure that nobody could fight that many, and he knew that I would soon be gone.

The dossier had clearly been built up over a period of time. Whilst it was happening, I was confused - angry, even - but it is only with the benefit of hindsight that I can truly appreciate how scared they were that something would go wrong. I would walk into a room full of patients with my white cane, naively not quite recognising the impact that it would have on them recognising the level of sight loss which I was suffering.

Some of the complaints were over misunderstandings, or over relatively minor issues bordering on nit-picking.

When someone is out to get you, they'll always find something to complain of. One of the complaints related to a dental antibiotic, metronidazole, which is used to treat various infections. When a patient is taking metronidazole, they mustn't drink alcohol because it can cause various unpleasant side-effects. On one occasion I'd prescribed metronidazole. The patient left the room, and I instantly realised that I'd forgotten to warn him about not drinking alcohol - so I followed him out, and told him. The dental nurse didn't overhear me telling him, so it went into the dossier of complaints as though Mr.Skipworth had failed to tell a patient that they couldn't drink alcohol.

Just think about that for a moment: if you were a nurse working as part of a team, what would you do in that situation? Surely you'd offer a quiet reminder to the dentist, or say something. On the other hand, if you were trying to build a case against someone, you'd be reporting it.

I don't blame the nurses, of course. They'd clearly been told to keep an eye on me, and to report anything and everything that they could to management. It just created an environment in which it was impossible to function without a constant feeling of being judged.

On another occasion, the computers (and we're talking about the old-fashioned kind which would break at the drop of a hat) weren't working. I had a patient who I knew well, and who I'd treated before. I knew precisely which teeth I was supposed to be working on, so rather than waste a patient's time rescheduling an appointment I just got on and did my job. Everyone was happy, but predictably the incident landed in the portfolio of complaints: "he never looked at the screen to check that these were the right teeth to take out". I knew the patient, I knew the teeth, and I could see for myself which teeth needed taking out.

At that point, I was seeing a lot of patients with special needs - often patients in wheelchairs, or with MS. They were in the 'disabled world', as we would have thought of it at the time. They understood, and I could discuss my problems with them. These patients were completely confident in my ability to treat them, because they knew from first-hand experience how wonderfully well human beings are able to adapt to changing circumstances and situations. It's remarkable how resilient we are, in a way - but it was the able-bodied people who didn't have the same level of tolerance and understanding. Even today, after all of the ups and downs of the last few years, I am sure that (as a one-off) I would be perfectly able to perform dental treatment using loupes. It wouldn't be practical of course, for many reasons, because of my general health and stamina. I'm perfectly happily retired.

On one of Michael Palin's travel programmes, he was travelling through India. He wanted to have a proper shave, and went to see someone in the streets of Bombay who was completely blind. The man gave him the perfect shave with a cut-throat razor - from feel alone.

At the height of all the difficulties, I went to take a bit of a break from everything - and to have a bit of a moan to one of my friends. We headed down to the local pub for a pint and to drown a few sorrows. It hadn't really twigged with me by this stage just how fully-sighted people were perceiving my work.

"Well, how much can you see, Bill?"

"I'm completely blind in my right eye, and I have some sight

loss at the bottom of my left eye."

Looking at me over his pint glass, he responded:

"Bill. I wouldn't want you treating my teeth with those eyes."

The penny dropped.

I was now suspended from work. Months went by, and my eyesight was deteriorating further - partly, perhaps, with the stress of the uncertainty of the situation. Too much eyesight had now gone, and I accepted that my health was too bad to be able to continue to work, so I applied for ill-health retirement.

I then received a letter informing me I was to be sacked due to issues of health and incompetence. I accepted the health part, but where was the incompetence? To me this was an obvious injustice, and I felt that I needed to fight it: I was going to take them to court for unfair dismissal. The issue wasn't whether I could do my job, but the damage to my name and reputation.

This period of my life felt like pure hell: over a successful thirty year dental career. I had built up a good name in the profession. I had genuine respect from colleagues and patients, and now I was judged as being incompetent and sacked. In the meantime, I was granted the ill-health retirement. I'd been concerned that I could be left with absolutely nothing, if I'd been sacked with no possibility of the retirement despite thirty years of service.

The whole process from when I was suspended in March 2007 was finally completed in December 2009. There had been delay after delay, partly causing by the clinic having lost all of my medical notes.

I put considerable time, energy and effort into defending the allegations of incompetence - whilst of course understanding that I could not continue in my work. I literally lived and breathed the case. In a lot of ways, it took two and a half years of my life away.

The Judge's verdict was that I had been unfairly dismissed, and I was awarded a modest amount of financial compensation. In the end I questioned if I should have gone through all of this, but I did get justice and in my official dental record with the British Dental Association it was made clear that I had left dentistry due to severe sight loss and not because of incompetence. I felt that I had been exonerated. The financial award mattered little to me: restoring my professional reputation was far more significant.

I went home, with three large black bin bags full of documents related to my case. I loaded them all onto a large bonfire. The relief was fantastic. Everything that had happened to me over the last two and a half years was gone. I watched the worries literally burn away in front of my eyes.

Chapter 7 - Synaesthesia

"I fused the beauty of dreaming and the reality of life into a single blissful colour...on a clear bright day even the softness of the sounds is golden" - Fernando Pessoa

All the way back in 1690, John Lock - the 'father of liberalism' and an Oxford academic whose theories of the mind are still studied to this day - wrote about a blind man who could sense the colour scarlet when he heard the sound of a trumpet.

When one sense triggers another in these unusual ways, it's known as synaesthesia. Popular culture has a particular fascination with synaesthesia, with numerous televised documentaries on the subject. People might perceive letters and numbers as having particular colours, sounds might trigger a physical sensation, or a certain taste appear in their mouth when they hear a particular word.

I suppose that the fascination comes from the fact that it's so alien to most people's understanding. The thought that sight, smell, touch, taste and hearing could be connected in ways which they're unaware of is different and utterly baffling to many people: it is something about our innate human curiosity, our desire to further our understanding of the universe in which we live.

In my case, synaesthesia began when my right eye went completely blind. I was playing around on the piano keyboard one day, when I was suddenly hit by a sensation which I can only describe as *light itself* - a bright light as I played the note of C at the top end of the piano.

I progressed down the scale of C: C, B, A, G, F, E, D, C. As I did so, remarkably the notes went to a yellow colour. I contiinued further, and as I reached the notes in the bass clef, it was more of a darker yellow.

Looking back now, the best explanation I can think of for this sudden change is that the eye uses a lot of neurones in the brain. My right eye no longer had anything to do, because there was no sight going through there. I imagine that the neurones in my brain needed to find a new expression, and perhaps tapped into some subconscious association which had already developed in my brain but had not yet had any opportunity to be triggered.

With different scales, I found that there would be corresponding linked emotions. In the key of C, I felt a bizarre sense of inexplicable joy and simplicity. Children's songs are often written in the key of C, possibly because it's the simplest to learn to play.

The great composer Mozart, as a young child, wrote the music for the song '*Twinkle Twinkle Little Star*'. The beautiful yet childish simplicity of that song is precisely what has made it a timeless hit with children across many countries, spanning a few centuries already.

There's a certain childishness within me, I suppose: something inside me instinctively warms to the key of C and to that same simplicity and gentleness. I'm often drawn back to Twinkle, Twinkle Little Star. I treat it as a basic, simple theme - and then compose all kinds of variations and harmonies on that theme, much in the same way as a jazz musician will improvise various riffs rather than sticking religiously to the music as written. There's something quite liberating about such improvisation, and it's one of the great joys of playing music.

Thinking back now, I wonder sometimes how much the conditions necessary for the synaesthesia were always there, hidden away deep in the recesses of my mind, and whether it would have remained there completely undiscovered if it were not for my sight loss. Some keys are 'clearer' to me than others: C, F and G were immediately obvious to me, whereas some of the other keys were a little more of a mystery. Perhaps that's something to do with experience: C,

F and G are relatively common keys for music to be written in (F and G having only one flat and one sharp respectively), so perhaps my experience and understanding of those keys is somewhat greater.

I switched to the key of F, which gave a sense of the colour blue. I played down the 'scale' - but only playing the white notes on the keyboard, known as a 'mode' of the original scale of C. As I came down, one note at a time, the blue would gradually become darker and darker until I found myself reaching the bass clef notes. Again, beginning with G, I found that the same pattern repeated - only this time, the colour was green, heading from a bright lime green for the high notes to a dark, forest green for the lower.

The others didn't come so easily to me: like the eye itself, it required a little more focus and interpretation: like when a baby is born, and it takes time for their experience to catch up with all the new and exciting shapes they can now see. It was something which would only truly come when I had more experience of the sensations associated with my synaesthesia. Each of the modes I've mentioned so far still sounded happy, like a melodic or 'major' key.

There's a sadness associated with minor keys: indeed, one of the most basic lessons of songwriting is that a 'happy' song should be composed in a major key, and a 'sad' song in a minor key. Like with any such rules across many walks of life, a genius might well be able to break the rules from time time time - but a beginner should follow them carefully. It's no surprise, then, that major keys elicit happy emotions and minor keys draw out sad ones.

Since that time, with greater experience, I've had time to go back and try to put the other 'modal' scales into sharper focus. Starting from A, I get a sense of the colour purple. From D, the colour is more of a reddy orange. E has a dark, miserable sense: it's a muddy colour, the kind of muddy-brown that you might get when trying to mix various colours together. That probably isn't a surprise either: the 'modal' scale of E, playing it without any black notes at all, is so far away from the key of E Major (which has four black notes) that it's not surprising there's some dissonance.

When I go back and play the actual scales of D and E Major, including the sharps, they both have the red/orange colour. I can make a little sense of that too: they start in similar places, both have sharps rather than flats, and are often used in marching music. Perhaps that's why I get this sense of brightness, of joy, and maybe even triumph. Those keys have something vibrant, positive and uplifting - but it's joyful in a very, very different sense to the key of C. Perhaps the greatest composers had an innate understanding, an ability to 'tap into' the human emotional response to music in ways which the rest of us cannot even begin to comprehend.

When I move to more unusual keys, I get the sense that I'm reaching the edge of the range of normal eyesight: the scale of B major, with five sharps, is peculiar and completely unique. Without the black notes, it would be atonal and miserable - but with the five sharps, it has a sense of majesty to me: an indigo or a violet.

I was once talking to a completely blind man in a barber's shop who played the piano. He had, at one point, had the ability to see so he could perceive what the colours were. We began to discuss music and the topic of synaesthesia came up. I was surprised, and more than a little intrigued, to learn that he had an experience almost identical to my own. I told him of how I perceived C major, and he agreed that there was a sense of a bright light. We shared our views of F and G as being blue and green respectively. I found it difficult to believe that I'd finally found someone else who could relate to my experience so closely. Having said that, I am perfectly well aware that synaesthesia varies dramatically from one person to another. Some composers might well associate notes with colours, but they could 'see' different colours to the ones that I would see.

Either way, I find that it often helps me when it comes to writing music. Almost like a painting, when I'm playing a piece of music I might well sense that a little dash of red, or blue, would make everything work better, and play the corresponding note on the piano. I remember giving a talk on my synaesthesia once, demonstrating it with a tune on a piano. A girl who must have been around the age of 11 came up to me afterwards, with a huge grin on her face, having connected to what I was saying and intuitively understanding perfectly what I meant. An older man in his 60s hadn't the faintest clue, feeling that it all came across as total gibberish to him.

Even though I've got some of my sight back, the synaesthesia is still progressing. The more unusual notes and scales are starting to take shape in my mind, and they are the most beautiful - and fascinating - of all. If I start with F# [F sharp], playing all the black notes, it is the most wonderful colour: one that cannot even be seen physically or described. Some of the most wonderfully beautiful songs are written in F# major. It is, to me, a *heavenly* colour. Our eyes can only see colours within a certain spectrum. Animals as diverse as butterflies and reindeer can see in ultraviolet light in ways which humans cannot.

I wonder whether, perhaps, when I visualise the colour which is associated in my mind with F# Major, I am able to 'see' a colour that's outside the visible spectrum itself. It's the same when starting on any of the black notes: I see incredible - indescribable - colours.

It is a gift which I find almost impossible to describe, and one which I am immeasurably grateful to have. I can hardly begin to scratch the surface of explaining them: I can say only that they are *beautiful,* and that they give me out-of-this-world, heavenly feelings.

Chapter 8 - Into Darkness

"Here is joy that cannot be shaken. Our light can swallow up your darkness; but your darkness cannot now infect our light"
- C.S. Lewis

There's something surprisingly calming about the Sheffield Supertram, gliding effortlessly along the rails between stops. I was sitting on the tram on a particularly unremarkable Friday afternoon, when my peaceful thoughts were suddenly interrupted:

"Go to the Eye Department at the Hallamshire Hospital now"

We all get that 'inner voice', I think: the sense of feeling that there is something we ought to do in a particular situation. That inner voice and conscience have an odd relationship; as a Christian, I believe that the Holy Spirit often works through that inner voice. On this occasion, though, the voice made little sense - except that it was stronger, more powerful, magnified as though my inner voice were speaking through a microphone. I argued: it's Friday afternoon, it's really busy now, and anyway I haven't got an eye problem.

"Go to the Eye Department at the Hallamshire Hospital now"

At around this time my eyesight had somewhat stabilised. I'd got involved with the blind and visually impaired community in Sheffield, becoming a radio presenter and doing a two-hour show every Tuesday afternoon. I joined a visually impaired writing group, and played the piano for many charity fundraising events. By this time, both my sons were grown up and had left home: life was good again, and the nightmare of my unfair dismissal case nothing but a distant memory. There was no reason to suppose that anything was out of the ordinary. I was comfortable.

"Go to the Eye Department at the Hallamshire Hospital now"

My heart sank. I knew that I would be waiting for hours if I headed over there. I had little choice: I succumbed to the inevitable and made my way across. Sure enough, when I arrived at the Clinic it was completely packed with some thirty of forty people. I waited for about three hours, and as it turned out I was the last to be seen that day. I even remember saying to her "I don't know why I'm here, because I feel fine".

In my sighted eye, the pressure was usually about 15. When your eyesight is going, you tend to become obsessed with glaucoma intraocular pressures. In my own mind, I was happy enough when it wasn't above 15. If it hits 20, they start to worry - and a pressure of 11 or 12 would indicate that I was doing really well. If the pressure is high, it squashes the retina and it can be permanent if it goes on for very long. On this occasion, the doctor tested the eye pressure and she went white - completely shocked to find that it was over 40. She immediately rushed me onto the ward upstairs and gave me some injections to bring the pressure down. She managed to get it down to 20. We both knew it was essential to get the pressure down, or I would go totally blind permanently.

I was completely dependent on that eye, so I was an especially urgent case. An emergency appointment was made for the following Monday to see a new glaucoma specialist. The more that I thought about that inner voice, the more astounded I was. I'd had no pain, no discomfort, and no further sight loss. There was no human, natural clue which could possibly explain how I had suddenly known that I needed to go.

The following Monday I met my new doctor, who I jokingly referred to as Doctor Gold (because the first two letters of his actual name were Au, the chemical symbol for gold). He radiated youth, vigour, and an encouraging and refreshing can-do attitude. The trabeculectomy done in my left eye was now failing. That operation normally worked for only ten years, but it had thankfully lasted for fifteen - and unbeknownst to me, in that time there was now a new treatment for glaucoma called a silicone implant. I was booked in for the operation as a matter of urgency, but my blood pressure was found to be too high. Eventually this pressure was stabilised, and I was booked in as an urgent case less than a week later.

Doctor Gold was doing the operation and I enjoyed jokingly telling people that my life was going to be transformed by a silicone implant: classic misdirection, as 'silicone implants' automatically made the mind wander in the direction of a 'boob job'. Apparently it's like a group of silicone tubes, which they put into the eye to automatically drain away the excess fluid.

Unlike the second trabeculectomy operation, I had no discomfort or irritation in the eye after it had been done. Because there is no 'bleb', it looks completely normal and all of the difficulty sleeping had gone overnight. The operation was a total success, and is still working to this day. A couple of weeks later, I had the pressure checked and it was now 12, which was absolutely spot on, and a bit different to 40. I could tell Doctor Gold was very pleased with the result. However, he warned me that a mild cataract I had in this eye would worsen because of the eye surgery. I couldn't believe how amazing this new treatment for glaucoma was: it was so much better than the old treatment, but the surgery in this left eye by the Irish doctor had lasted far longer than I'd originally expected.

As the weeks went by, my sight had became very poor as Doctor Gold had warned me. I could tell it wasn't related to do with the glaucoma. Imagine that you're rubbing a pencil drawing away that you've just done. With glaucoma, it feels like the thing which I could see before had just disappeared.

A cataract, on the other hand, is more like a dense fog. You're aware that there is something there, but it's clouded by the fog. In the horror film 'The Fog', all kind of bad things happen in a dense, ubiquitous fog. It's a bit like living through that. I could still see colours and shapes, light and dark, but the whole effect was like looking through a fogged-up dirty window.

Soon I couldn't see well enough to read, then I couldn't see well enough to make a cup of tea, and very quickly I descended into total blindness. I would describe my blindness as like lots of doors being shut. There seemed to be endless tasks which to a sighted person are nothing, but to a blind person become almost impossible. Over a few months, my sight had now completely gone.

The first door to be slammed shut was while eating food. My wife gave me a plate of food with a knife and fork, and I found these were completely unusable. Within half an hour my food was all ddsfsdover me, on the floor, and on my seat. We both quickly worked out that the best way to feed me was by having a large bowl and spoon on a tray. Eating a slice of pizza with my fingers was brilliant, and any finger foods were easy to eat.

Early on, I went into the kitchen to get myself a bowl of cornflakes. I didn't know exactly where the cornflakes were, but being blind I could no longer distinguish between different boxes. I had to open each box, and use my sense of touch to figure out which of the contents felt like cornflakes. Then, I had to feel around to find a bowl - but I didn't know how many cornflakes I was putting into the bowl, so it all overflowed. I had to try to remove some of the excess cornflakes. Finding the milk was difficult in the fridge, but I had no idea whether I'd put enough milk into the bowl or too much. I finally, after a lot of effort, had just about managed to get myself a bowl of cornflakes. By the time my wife came home, however, she came back to milk and cornflakes all over the counter and all over the floor. I realised just how little I was now able to do for myself.

Doing my daily crossword was another door that closed. I could no longer read anything, so I couldn't read any books any more. Even something as simple as plugging in an electrical appliance became impossible: I couldn't line the plug up with the socket.

When you're blind, you don't know where exactly you are in the room. It mean that, even though I had been living in the house for nearly twenty years, I had very little concept of where I actualy was. Over time, I was able to develop some coping mechanisms by learning how to feel my way around. People who have been blind since birth are used to such things; going blind after having had some eyesight means that you have to adjust your entire way of thinking. Touch and fingers become the most wonderful things ever. That's why I say that finger food is so amazing: the textures become part of the experience of eating, and there's no need to attempt to use a knife and fork. In the end I worked out that the furry scatter rug was in front of the fireplace. From there, I was able to deduce that my back was to the fireplace and I now had a point of reference so that I knew where everything else was in the room. Such techniques were helpful to me, but it also all created a total sense of dependency.

Crossing a road without a sighted guide was dangerous. Blindness had took away so much of my life. I couldn't see flowers or people's faces anymore: so much of the beauty that we take for granted in everyday life had been extinguished. I really didn't feel I could cope, but at the same time certain things were still intact. I could still enjoy listening to (and playing) beautiful music. I could hear the radio, listen to stories, have good conversations, and I could smell lots of interesting scents - as well as taste and smell delicious food.

On one day I went to Wetherspoons with some friends, and needed to use the toilet. I hadn't realised until then how much of a problem even going to the toilet would be when out of the house. Because I was blind, I couldn't see where to aim. I was so embarrassed that I zipped myself up and ran out. From that day on, I had to sit down to use the toilet. It doesn't sound like much, in comparison with some of the other struggles, I felt, in some sense, emasculated by that experience: my inability to use the toilet like anyone else had become a kind of metaphor for the struggles caused by my blindness.

In truth, I was struggling to cope and so was my wife. Even getting into a car became a big issue. I wouldn't know which way the car was facing, so wouldn't know which way round to sit in the car. I would regularly bump my head getting in the car. Our marriage was becoming impossible, and I knew that if I didn't get my sight back soon it would cause us both huge problems, as it was causing an immense strain on both of us and our relationship.

Chapter 9 - Charles Bonnet Syndrome

"Not for a moment do I take you for a truth that is real", Ivan exclaimed in what even amounted to fury. "You are a falsehood, you are my illness, you are a ghost. Only I do not know how to destroy you, and perceive that for a certain time I must suffer you. You are a hallucination I am having" - Fyodor Dostoyevsky, The Brothers Karamazov

A couple of weeks after my silicone implant operation, my blindness was just beginning. I was sitting in my chair in the living room, and at this point I could still just barely make out the patio windows.

Out of the edge of my eye, I clearly saw two Victorian children - arm in arm - sitting in a toboggan. They came in straight through the patio window and out again, riding up and down on the grass outside. They had their arms around each other and were obviously enjoying themselves. I saw one of them had a mop of ginger curls, blue eyes, and a ruddy complexion. She looked a bit like Shirley Temple. The whole thing lasted about twenty minutes, and it was like watching a video being played out, but in total silence.

It was my first experience of a visual hallucination, and I actually quite enjoyed watching it. Surprisingly, perhaps, I didn't think so much of it at the time. It hadn't been a particularly frightening experience, and indeed it had been rather relaxing, so I was not at all disturbed and thought little more about it. Charles Bonnet Syndrome had been triggered by severe sight loss, but I had no idea what was coming.

A few days later, my wife took me out for a drive. As we drove through Sheffield, it was like driving through a war zone. All the houses looked bombed out and destroyed, and the road appeared to be strewn with bricks and mortar. As we drove up the hill, it felt like we were driving vertically straight upwards, and as though we were about to drop off a vertical surface.

As we drove into Derbyshire, on the winding country roads, I felt the car was on a 45-degree incline. I feared that if she stopped driving, the car would fall into a deep chasm which I could see. We were driving to Castleton, and the road was lined with trees and greenery - but to me it was completely disorienting, almost like riding on one of the scariest rides at Alton Towers.

As I got out of the car in Castleton, I felt a little shaken. The horror continued. Walking on the footpath, my mind conjured up deep crevasses on either side, and if my foot slipped off the path I would fall to my death into the crevasse. I held onto my wife's arm as if my life depended on it. I asked if she would take me to the cafe for a cup of tea. She led me in, and tried to sit me down on a vacant seat. Unfortunately, my mind had conjured up a rather large (think: Hyacinth Bucket in Keeping Up Appearances) lady sitting in that seat - and I was convinced that my wife was trying to push me into her lap. My wife and I had a push-me, pull-you fight in the middle of the cafe - and eventually she manged to sit me down in the chair where the 'lady' was sitting. The moment I sat down on the chair, she disappeared: she had never, of course, really existed. Everything about that trip had been horrific.

I soon learned to trust my wife completely. If I had believed my hallucinations, my wife would have appeared to be leading me into brick walls, fences, and garage doors. However, as she led me through the so-called danger, it would disappear. One day we went to Meadowhall and I was convinced the roof was about half an inch above my head and that at any moment I would bang my head on it.

There's a Charles Bonnet Syndrome group at the Royal Society for the Blind, so fortunately it didn't take very long for me to realise that is what was happening. I knew that I wasn't struggling with a major psychiatric disorder. The ability to recognise that such hallucinations aren't real is something which indicated that I wasn't, in fact, losing my mind. Some people are naturally better than others at learning to ignore these strange, confusing pieces of information. It's certainly something which makes you think: fragments of images. Perhaps it's something about the subconscious mind, offering a warning about the sight loss - or perhaps that my eyes weren't doing anything, so my brain was plucking random things out of the air.

I do find it strange that some of those visions are of things which would actually have happened: Victorian children tobogganing, or a desolate Sheffield having been bombed out in the blitz.

Charles Bonnet Syndrome is quite common amongst people who suffer sight loss. It's well known, and well documented, today - but back in Victorian times, it was seen as a sign of derangement. People would be put into what they called 'mental asylums'. I could tell that my wife was particularly concerned by what I was seeing.

In my case it only lasted a few months, and it never returned once I'd managed to get my eyesight back, but it was an extraordinary - and terrifying - period of my life.

Chapter 10 - My chains fell off

"My chains fell off, my heart was free, I rose, went forth, and followed thee"

- John Wesley, And Can It Be

I was now completely distraught, feeling lost in my own home despite having lived there for over twenty years. I could see absolutely nothing except for the hallucinations, and eating - in the emotional state I was in at the time - felt as though I was eating from a pig's trough. It's perhaps the complete reliance upon other people which was the most debilitating of all.

I went to see Dr Gold in a totally blind state, and it appeared to all the world as though the silicone implants had failed. Thankfully, though, he was able to offer me a ray of hope: he assured me that my blindness was all caused by the dense cataract, and that once the cataract was removed I would be able to see again - as well as I had done for years. However, in order to avoid damaging the implants, he had to wait a few months for them to settle into the eye before removing the cataract. I would have to stay blind until the date of the operation, and it would be one of the most difficult periods of waiting of my whole life.

A date was set for the cataract operation: November 11th, at 11am. I had been finally offered a ray of hope: I knew that there was a date on which my blindness would come to an end, and I had no reason to doubt his word. I was just living for that day, November 11th, which coincidentally was

Armistice Day - celebrating the end of the Great War and the cessation of hostilities. There were still a couple more setbacks, but I was on the path to regaining my eyesight - and with it, an end to the Charles Bonnet hallucinations.

The fateful day came. Nothing was ever simple: the power failed, and a cacophony of fire alarms rang out across the hospital. Operations were being cancelled left, right and centre as chaos reigned. Dr Gold came to visit me, and took pity on me. He assured me that if he could find a slot he would treat me as a priority and make sure to do the operation that day: he knew just how desperate I was to get my sight back. Eventually, later that afternoon, I was wheeled into the theatre and Dr Gold performed the cataract operation on my left eye.

Everyone had told me that my sight would be restored immediately, but after the operation the blindness was exactly the same. It was another hammer-blow of devastation.

By the following morning I was having to accept that the operation hadn't worked, but then I heard the same inner voice speaking to me again - the one which had told me to go to the hospital in the first place. The words I heard were strange, and concerning.

"Yes, you are going to get some of your sight back - but you are to give it away to three totally blind friends immediately"

At this point, I should offer some explanation. There's a passage in the Bible, which many people find incredibly difficult to understand. Halfway through the book of Genesis, God tells Abraham to offer his son Isaac as a sacrifice. Abraham had waited many years to have his son, and to be asked to kill him seemed horrific, terrifying and wrong. Yet of course God never intended for Abraham to kill his own son: it was a test - was Abraham willing to give up the one thing in life so precious to him, knowing that God himself was more important? When Abraham demonstrated his willingness to pass the test, God intervened - and of course, Isaac was unharmed.

I feel very strongly that this time in my life was intended as being such a test. I had lost my sight. I knew just how terrible and terrifying that was - but was I prepared, truly prepared, to put other people first? That thought, that inner voice, didn't actual make practical sense: eyesight is hardly a commodity to be transferred from one person to another! Did I demonstrate that willingness? As a Christian, I'm told to put others first: in Philippians 2:3-4 I'm told *"Do nothing out of selfish ambition or vain conceit. Rather, in humility value others above yourselves, not looking to your own interests but each of you to the interests of the others"*.

Sometimes that's easy to do. What happens, though, when the challenge is greater, when you're asked to lay down something which is of pivotal importance to you? My initial reaction wasn't great: I screamed out in my head "No way"!

I had already been blind for four months, and I wasn't prepared to be blind any longer. Yet still it persisted, the challenge in my mind. For the whole day on Saturday I was continually tormented with this request. Finally, that evening, I gave in - and said to myself "Okay, I give in, give this sight to them and I'll stay blind for the rest of my life". As I accepted that, suddenly I felt a heavy burden lift away from my shoulders. I felt an inexplicable sense of peace and fell into a deep sleep.

I woke up on the Sunday morning. I could see my hands and fingers for the first time in months. I examined my hands, noticing my gold wedding ring on my third finger. Excited, I rushed to the curtains and opened them. I was overwhelmed by the sight of the blue sky, the sunshine, the doors and windows of the houses. The dense fog I had lived with for months had lifted. I was ecstatic: I could see!

I could see my wife's face again, her beautiful eyes, the green grass. The whole of the day was filled with pure joy and delight. I walked straight out of the house and into the car. I got into it easily. It was in sharp contrast to recent months: when I was blind, I struggled to get into the car - and the Charles Bonnet Syndrome had always been particularly bad for some reason during a car journey. My wife's face was a picture of astonishment as I got in the front seat with no problem. That afternoon as we drove into Derbyshire, I saw a very bare tree. All the leaves had dropped off in the autumn gloom, but to me that tree was the most beautiful tree ever.

I was overcome with emotion and tears of joy were coursing down my face. We went to the Strine's Inn for a coffee. The roaring real fire lapped up the logs in the fireplace, details which I could see clearly. Every little detail became so precious to me: the pattern of frothy milk on the top of my latte with the spoon sticking out; the movement of the spoon in the coffee. Never had I appreciated such mundane things as being so glorious, yet these little patterns all over our natural world have a charming and detailed beauty of their own - one which we can easily miss in the clutter of a modern world.

The next few days were moments of total joy and happiness, as many things that before had been so difficult and hard had now become easy. A few months earlier, thick iron doors had been repeatedly slammed shut on my world. Now, they had been blown wide open once more; light and possibilities were pouring through. It was the little things as much as the big things: getting a bowl of cornflakes was now easy! I could see the cornflake packet, I could pour the cornflakes into the bowl, pour the milk in until there was enough and find a spoon in the drawer immediately.

I could put my CD player on easily, and put the three-pin plug in the socket. I could see my music on the piano and began to play properly again with no problem. I had continual joy and satisfaction.

I could also see the piles of dead leaves on the autumn pavement, having great fun kicking them in the air in a way that a young child might. I had missed the golden-brown hues and colours of a beautiful autumn day, but now I was making up for lost time.

I went to the toilets in Wetherspoons. I swaggered up to the urinal, unzipped myself and watched the urinary flow. I aimed it directly into the urinal with a great deal of satisfaction. I was now a man again, doing what men do.

When I went again to see Dr Gold, the difference from my last visit when I was totally blind was incredible. Nobody could fail to notice the transformation: I could see the chair to sit in, and I could see and read most of the letters on his eye chart. As I shook his hand, I had the sense of just how inadequate that was as a means of saying 'thank you': Dr Gold had given me my sight back. I felt as though he deserved a million pounds, and even that wouldn't feel enough somehow for the gift of sight. I can only express my enormous gratitude for the skill and expertise of everyone at the Royal Hallamshire.

Typically, Dr Gold was totally humble about the amazing results of his surgical skill. As a token of my appreciation, I gave him a picture which I had drawn some years earlier of a cat peeping out from under a duvet cover. He put it up in his surgery, which I was very pleased about. On the page, in black and white, the detail may not quite be fully visible to you.

The words of the hymn Amazing Grace spring to mind, almost as an anthem describing my journey - both spiritual and physical:

"Amazing Grace, how sweet the sound

That saved a wretch like me

I once was lost, but now am found,

*Was blind, but **now I see**"*

Chapter 11 - It's in my DNA

"We have the DNA of our Lord Jesus Christ"
- Herschel Walker, former NFL running back
and Olympic athlete

There are times when even some of my closest friends and family don't understand why I often talk about my faith. Yet my Christianity is an integral part of me, more pivotal to my life than anything else - including my eyesight. It's every bit as important to the person I am as my very DNA. In writing this book, I'd been planning to write mainly about my faith in this chapter. But a lot of the events contained within it just don't make any sense at all without linking them to my faith.

Were it not for my faith, I might well have been killed during my time at university. Were it not for my faith, I would likely never have become a dentist. Were it not for my faith, I might not have met my wife. Were it not for my faith, I would not have known to go to the Hallamshire hospital eye department at just the right time - and I'd likely be completely blind today, unable to write this book.

But more than any individual incident, my faith underpins my character and motivation. It's true that the Bible, in the Great Commission, tells me that I should share the 'good news' of Jesus Christ with other people. That doesn't necessarily mean the old-fashioned preachers standing outside with a placard urging us all to repent - far from it! It means that Christians should take the opportunities which happen to arise from time to time to share it. If I'd learned anything else - from any field other than religious belief - which I believed to be great news for someone dear to me, of course I would share it. Why would I not do the same about my Christian belief? So whilst in one sense I do very much hope that nobody would take offence at me telling you about who I am, in another sense I can make no apology for it.

I can't prove to you who Jesus is, or that the truths contained within the Bible are in fact eternal truths of great importance, but I can only speak from my own experience and act as a witness to show (despite the fact that there are mysteries which I may never understand) how He has transformed my life already, and how that process continues. I am very much a 'work in progress', with many rough edges still needing to be smoothed off, but I know that He is transforming my life still.

Unlike many people growing up in the early 1960s, I didn't have much of a background of Christianity at the junior school I attended. There was no particular religious character to the assemblies, and none of the hymn-singing which is stereotypically associated with that period.

At the age of around 7, I recall being asked by my teacher to draw something about Easter. The examples given were a bunny or an egg, but for some reason I drew a cross. I didn't know what it meant - just that it was 'something to do with Easter', without having any idea of why.

Years later, after I'd become a Christian, my mum found this drawing of a cross and brought it out to show me. Something had obviously been bubbling up inside me: God must have had his hand on my life even when I was young.

The headmaster, at that time, was a Communist and very anti-Christian. There was not even a whisper of anything about God whatsover: it was complete silence, nothing.

There was one notable exception: a Christmas play at my junior school which I remember well. The concept was that aliens had come down from another planet, and wanted to know what Christmas was about.

Coincidentally, I had the main part: that of a poet who had been kidnapped by aliens, and who had to explain the meaning of Christmas to them. It gave me the opportunity (though I didn't fully know or understand it myself) to share a large part of the good news with all the school, parents and grandparents who had come to watch. The whole situation was ironic because my passion was evangelism - sharing the good news - when I became a Christian.

During my first year at secondary school, the whole lesson was about the pots and ruins in ancient times in Israel and Palestine - yet not a single word of information about any of the events underpinning those times. My ignorance was profound - so much so that, at the age of 20 when I became a Christian, I had no concept whatsoever of who the Apostle Paul was.

As an older teenager, whilst I was at sixth form college, I started experimenting with alcohol and arriving back home late at night. Surprisingly enough, because he was quite a tough man, my dad was getting concerned and telling me that I needed to stop doing it. He kept saying to me, again and again, "why do you think I am doing this?"

He obviously wanted me to respond by saying "because you love me". But for some reason I couldn't say the word "love" - I would respond "because you like me" or "because you like me a lot". At that time, I didn't feel as though I had any love in me: I didn't feel as though I loved him or anyone at all. He kept asking the same question again. I actually ended up going back to my room, before coming back and finally saying in a begrudging way "because you love me". Like many teenagers, I suppose I was struggling with expressing my emotions in any way at all. But the whole thing rather mirrored the Bible story where Jesus asked Peter "Do you love me?" three times, and Peter had to respond three times.

The passage doesn't translate properly into English from the original Greek in which it's written. We have just one word for 'love', which carries different meanings depending on ths context. In Ancient Greek, there were four:

Agape - the all-encompassing love which God has for us

Phileo - a strong friendship-type bond

Eros - sexual love

Storge - an affinity, like you might "love" the countryside

Jesus asked Peter "Do you love (agape, all-encompassing) me?" And Peter responded "Yes Lord, you know that I love (I quite like) you." That's why Jesus asked the question again and again, trying to elicit a stronger response from Peter. Each time, he responded by saying "I like you" rather than "I truly love you". When the question is asked and answered the third time, in the ancient Greek the different word for 'love' is used. I'm struck by that story, just because of how similar it is to my own situation with my dad.

At around that time, a vicar happened to be in my sixth form college. He said only one thing that was of any use, but it was a profound three words: "God is love". That night I knelt down by my bed and said "I believe in you, God of love". Something happened on that day. I realised that I believed in God, but understood nothing more than that. Even so, there was an instant change within me. I understood that I did have love for my mother and father, which flowed from the understanding that I had love for God.

That was, in effect, all I really understood about God by the time I went to university. I knew nothing of the Bible, just those three words: that God is love. When someone knocked on my door in the halls of residence and asked whether I would like to look at the Bible with him at a Bible study, I found it wonderful. Nobody had ever shown me anything about the Bible's teachings. He couldn't believe just how enthusiastically I wanted to read the Bible, but it was something which I'd always wanted to learn more about. He gave me a copy of the Gospel of John. Every word of it seemed to make sense, and as I reached the words in chapter 14 "I am the way, the truth and the life. No-one comes to the Father except through me", it hit me like a thunderbolt.

I was invited to a large evangelical Christian meeting known as 'Come together in Jesus' name'. I was delighted to get a seat on the front row. One of the songs repeated 'his name is Jesus, the mighty God'. I had the sudden realisation not just that it was true, but also that it required a response from me. Later I was taken to, of all places, a Welsh chapel in Reading, where we sang the hymn 'When I Survey the Wondrous Cross'. It harped back to everything from my childhood: the cross (which I had drawn at age 7), the 'love so amazing, so divine' (which was my understanding of God from sixth form), and then finishing with the words "demands my soul, my life, my all". It put the final piece into the jigsaw of the Gospel.

Yes, Jesus was - and is - God. Yes, He had sacrificed Himself on the cross for our sins and defeated death. Yes, His free gift is eternal life for all. But there was something more: a need for me to personally respond to it, a need for me to accept that gift because He would never force or coerce me into accepting it. I needed to make my choice freely, to say sorry for all of the bad things I had done - and instead,to ask Him to be at the centre of my life. I ran back to my room at the halls of residence, knelt down at my bed, and prayed. That was the day that I truly accepted Him into my life.

All of my other experiences flow from that day. The manifestation of my new-found faith came so soon after that, when I didn't go home to work at Flixborough after feeling that something wasn't quite right. Praying about the situation led to clarity, and that clarity led to me making the correct decision. The rest of my life can't be separated from my Christianity.

I felt very strongly that God had told me to stay where I was. However, it made no sense as I would need money to be able to live. I set off at around 8 o'clock on my bike to look for work. I found myself outside Courage's brewery, and there was a big notice on the door saying 'Jobs Available - Apply Within'. I thought that God couldn't possibly want me to work in a brewery, so I immediately rejected the opportunity that had been handed to me on a plate. By amazing coincidence (and such coincidences happen all the time to Christians) I got completely lost. Within quarter of an hour, I ended up back at exactly the same point outside exactly the same door. I knocked on the door, walked in, and asked about the jobs. It was the Friday, and they said that I could start straight away on the following Monday. I'd found myself a summer job in under an hour of hunting, and it didn't quite dawn on me until a few months later (when a friend had trouble getting the same job and said "Gone are the days when you could just walk in and get a job") just how unusual that really was. God had provided me with the alternative to working at Flixborough. That's what He does: He always has a plan, and there's always an alternative around the corner.

In a strange sort of way, my eyesight has been symbolic of my spiritual journey. I do not see fully. There have been times when I have been physically blind, times when I have seen only partly or seen everyday items as though they were surrounded by a dense fog. My eyes have been physically incapable of seeing everything clearly.

In much the same way, before I became a Christian I was spiritually blind: I knew that there existed some part of life which was spiritual. I knew that I believed in the existence of God, but I knew nothing about him. Over the years I have gradually learned more. I have gone from the darkness of knowing absolutely nothing about Him to the point where I now know some things. But I still do not see clearly; I think that it's impossible for a limited human being to fully grasp the nature of an infinite God.

In 1 Corinthians 13:12, the Bible describes us as seeing "through a glass darkly" (King James Version) or a "dim reflection in a mirror" (Berean Study Bible). But one day, I know that I'll be with Him. Then, I know that I will be able to 'see' fully.

"For now we see only a reflection as in a mirror; then we shall see face to face. Now I know in part; then I shall know fully, even as I am fully known" - 1 Corinthians 13:12 (New International Version)

Epilogue

I'm writing these words four years after my eyesight returned, towards the end of 2020. I still have regular check-ups, but unfortunately the glaucoma has taken a little bit more sight from the bottom edge of my sighted eye. However, in practical terms it has made no difference to my day to day life and I remain incredibly grateful for the gift of sight. The scarring on my blind eye has become very severe, caused by the laser-burning operation which has resulted in constant irritation. Apparently calcification has occurred in the scarring, and this needs to be removed to make it more comfortable.

Because of what has happened to me, I feel an incredible rapport with blind people. I have had a glimpse into the frustration and at times deep sadness that blindness brings with it. But then, most blind people - especially those born blind - have no self-pity whatsoever. They just get on with life as they find it, offering a real inspiration to sighted people if they could only see it.

Blind people need a lot of help and support, and I feel that I am uniquely placed to attempt to give that help and support. I am always amused by people with two eyes that play the national lottery. Don't they realise they are already multiple millionaires? They have two eyes that work, and

should be thankful for what they have. It's become so easy in our consumer-driven society to seek money or physical possessions, when those things really aren't the most important in life.

That doesn't mean that things are easy now, or indeed that my eyesight causes no problems. Recently, because of my sight loss, I didn't see a step outside, and fell head first onto some concrete and it knocked two of my front teeth out. I've had to spend time on the other side of the dentist's chair as a result, so my sight loss does raise it's ugly head now and again.

At times I do feel a sense of survivors' guilt when I am with my blind friends. Why is it that they are blind and I can see? Still, I have needed to accept the fact that I've recovered my eyesight and learned to use it to help my blind friends.

It is quite possible - likely even - that I might once again lose my remaining eyesight at some point in the future. If that happens, it happens - and it could end up being permanent rather than temporary. I see this time of sight as being a gift, and I'm determined to make the most that I can out of this gift. At the moment, the door of possibilities remains

wide open, The door of being able to tell stories will always be open, and I am enjoying the freedom of writing books and telling stories with the aim of making a difference in people's lives.

Finally, I thank God: the one who has always been faithful, throughout my life, and who I know will always continue to be faithful to me - both in this life, and in the next.

"Now to him who is able to do immeasurably more than all we ask or imagine, according to his power that is at work within us, to him be glory in the church and in Christ Jesus throughout all generations, for ever and ever! Amen." - Ephesians 3:20-21